The local search series

Editor: Mrs Molly Harrison MBE

The Theatre

An old-fashioned theatre, Princes Theatre, Shaftesbury Avenue, 1911.

The Theatre

Olive Ordish
Line drawings by Gwen Mandley

London Routledge & Kegan Paul

*First published 1972
by Routledge & Kegan Paul Ltd
Broadway House, 68–74 Carter Lane.
London EC4V 5EL
Photoset and printed by
BAS Printers Limited, Wallop, Hampshire
© Olive Ordish 1972
No part of this book may be reproduced in
any form without permission from the
publisher, except for the quotation of brief
passages in criticism
ISBN 0 7100 7223 6 (c)
ISBN 0 7100 7224 4 (l)*

The local search series

Editor: Mrs Molly Harrison MBE

Many boys and girls enjoy doing research about special topics and adding drawings, photographs, tape-recordings and other kinds of evidence to the notes they make. We all learn best when we are doing things ourselves.

The books in this series are planned to help in this kind of 'project' work. They give basic information but also encourage the reader to find out other things; they answer some questions but ask many more; they suggest interesting things to do, interesting places to visit, and other books that can help readers to enjoy their finding out and to look more clearly at the world around them.

M.H.

'. . . all the business of life is to endeavour to find out what you don't know by what you do'

John Whiting *Marching Song*

Contents

		page
	Editor's preface	viii
1	Introducing the theatre	1
2	Plays and playwrights	6
3	Construction	14
4	Production	21
5	Acting	28
6	Design	39
7	Lighting and other jobs in the theatre	46
8	History of the British theatre	51
9	Do-it-yourself theatre	61
10	Finance	64
	Aids to research and projects on the theatre	66
	Some useful books	67
	Glossary of technical terms used	68
	Acknowledgments	70

Editor's preface

Most people enjoy watching plays and many enjoy taking part in the varied activities connected with the theatre. Drama is one of the oldest interests of human beings, and this book may help you realize some of the reasons for this.

It is written to help you to get more enjoyment from seeing plays, reading them, acting in them and perhaps writing them. We usually enjoy things more when we can understand them better, and there are a great many things to learn about and to understand in the theatre.

If you are planning to do a project on the theatre, you will need to decide how you are going to present your work and how you are going to divide it up. This book is full of ideas about things to do, things to discuss and read and things to make, but you will also have to use your eyes and your imagination. You will need to talk about the theatre to people of different kinds and from different countries, to watch actors of all sorts and to think carefully about the varied ways of presenting a play, whether in a theatre, at school or on television. The theatre in England at the present time is renowned for the inventiveness of its writers, its actors and its producers.

You will, of course, want to arrange the information and ideas and pictures you collect in the best order — the headings and chapters in this book will serve as one guide, and your own ideas about arrangement are important too. Don't forget to make your work look as clear and pleasant as you can, and to include as many illustrations as possible. Remember that the theatre is a visual art.

M.H.

Introducing the theatre   1

Recent new theatres in England

The effects of drama upon people

Ideas about your project

Have you ever been to a 'live' theatrical performance? Television and cinema are near relations to the theatre, of course, but there is something special about seeing a play performed by living actors and actually happening as you watch. It is often said that there is a sort of magic in the theatre that makes people enjoy working there, although it can be a hard life with poor pay.
Go to a 'live' play if you get the chance and see if you agree. Sixty years ago that would not have been difficult, because there was a theatre then in every town of any size and companies of actors toured from place to place. But after the First World War some theatres closed and others were used for different purposes, just as many cinemas have now been turned into bingo halls. Can you think of one important reason why theatres were closing at that time?

Theatres of a new kind
'The theatre is dying', people began to say. But how wrong they were! In recent years many splendid new theatres have been built, like those in Chichester and Guildford. Other companies have altered old premises and used them for presenting plays. Some arts centres include a theatre, as at the Midland Arts Centre in Birmingham. At Billingham Arts Centre there is a library, a dance hall and an ice-rink as well as a theatre. And people, especially young people, are flocking to these places.
The Octagon Theatre in Bolton has a new theatre for its resident company and has a second group that travels about giving performances at schools.

Introducing the theatre

The towns marked on this map contain theatres. Can you fill in some more?

The National Theatre in London, which is using an ancient playhouse called the 'Old Vic' until its new building is ready, has recently started a second company called the 'Young Vic', just round the corner, which presents plays especially for young people up to the age of twenty-five, including children. People

Introducing the theatre

older than that have to pay twice as much if they want to come too. The Royal Shakespeare Company have something of the same sort in London's Theatre-go-Round.
Why is there so much new interest in the theatre? Perhaps it is because television has aroused our interest in drama. Or is it that young people have more money to spend? Think over what may be the reason for the theatre's new popularity.
Is there a theatre in your town? Where is your nearest theatre? In London there are about fifty theatres, so if you live there you have almost too much choice!

Drama all around us

Plays have been performed all through history and in every land. Acting and plays in one form or another seem to be very much a part of human nature. You know about children's 'pretending games', school plays, television, a Punch and Judy show, etc. How many other kinds of 'theatre' can you think of? Plays may express the author's thoughts about life. Sometimes they bring fresh ideas or add something to those we already have.
Drama is entertainment but it can be more than that. It can influence us deeply. Perhaps you have heard discussions about whether there is too much violence on television. Some say it gets us used to the idea of hurting people so that we mind it less in reality. Others think that watching make-believe violence gets rid of the real violent feelings inside us. What do you think about this? It could make a good subject for a debate (non-violent!) between you and your friends.
There are many different kinds of theatrical entertainment and shapes of stage as well as all sorts of jobs connected with the theatre. Not just acting but writing, painting, electrical work and carpentry. Think about how those jobs would help in putting on a play. Which would interest *you* most?

Your project

So you see that if you decide to make a project on the theatre there is enough subject matter to make five hundred projects and you will have to choose the aspect that interests you most. You could, for instance, do a project about the theatre in your

THEATRE ROYAL, COVENT GARDEN.

The Public is respectfully informed, that

Mr. KEAN

was last Thursday received in the character of SHYLOCK with acclamations;—and in order to meet the generally expressed desire that he should appear with his Son,

The Tragedy of OTHELLO

will be acted this evening,
when they will perform together, for the first time.

This present MONDAY, March 25, 1833, Shakspeare's Tragedy of

OTHELLO.

The Duke of Venice, Mr. RANSFORD,
Brabantio, Mr. DIDDEAR, Gratiano, Mr. TURNOUR,
Lodovico, Mr. PAYNE, Montano, Mr. HAINES,
Othello by Mr. KEAN,
Cassio, Mr. ABBOTT,
Iago, (first time) Mr. CHARLES KEAN,
Roderigo, Mr. FORESTER, Antonio, Mr. IRWIN, Julio, Mr. T. Matthews
Giovanni, Mr. J. COOPER, Luca, Mr. BRADY, Lorenzo Mr. Bender
Messenger Mr MEARS, Marco Mr Collet, Cosmo Mr Heath, Paolo MrStanley
Desdemona, (first time) Miss E. TREE,
Emilia, Mrs. LOVELL.

After which, (3d time) A NEW FARCE, in Two Acts, called

A Nabob for an Hour

Mr. Frampton, Mr. ABBOTT, Sam Hobbs, Mr. BARTLEY,
Dick Dumpy, Mr. KEELEY,
Emma Leslie, Miss SYDNEY, Nanny Scraggs, Mrs. KEELEY.

To conclude with the Grand Ballet of

MASANIELLO.

Masaniello, (Fisherman of Portici) Mons. COULON,
Alphonse, (Viceroy of Naples) Mons. THEODORE GUERINOT,
Pietro, Mr. PAYNE, Borella, Mr. GOURIET, Morino, Mr. MICHAU, Lasarini, Mr. T. MATTHEWS
Francisco, Mr. CHICKINI, Lazzaroni, Mr. ELLER, Lorenzo, Mr. IRWIN, Selva, Mr. BERTRAM
Fenella, (Sister of Masaniello) Madame PROCHE GIUBILEI,
Elvire, (Wife of Alphonse) Mlle. ADELE, Dame of Honour, Miss THORPE.

On this occasion, the Vocal Parts will be sustained by
Mess. WILSON, I. BENNETT, DURUSET, HENRY, MORLEY, G. PENSON, RANSFORD, STANSBURY
Mesdames H. CAWSE DALY, HORTON, INVERARITY, KEELEY, LEE, E. ROMER, SHIRREFF.
In act I. A PAS DEUX by Mons. THEODORE GUERINOT and Mlle. ADELE.
In act II. A BOLERO by MONS. COULON & MADAME PROCHE GIUBILEI.
A TARENTELLE by Mr. MICHAU and Mrs. VEDY.

PLACES for the BOXES to be had of Mr. NOTTER, at the Box-Office, Hart-Street, from Ten till Four

Auber's new Opera of

THE COINERS,

Or, The SOLDIER's OATH,

having been honoured with the most COMPLETE SUCCESS, and announced for repetition amidst general and enthusiastic applause, will be performed To-morrow & Saturday next, And Three Times a Week after Easter.

A NABOB FOR AN HOUR

having again been received with roars of laughter and applause, will be repeated

Every Evening until further notice.

Tomorrow, (2d time) AUBER's New Opera of **The COINERS, or the Soldier's Oath**
With (4th time) **A Nabob for an Hour.**
To conclude with (38th time) the new Drama of **NELL GWYNNE.**
On Wednesday, (Last Night but One) the highly popular New Dramatic Oratorio, called
The Israelites in Egypt; or, the Passage of the Red Sea.
On Easter-Monday will be produced, a New SERIO-COMIC LEGENDARY FAIRY TALE, (which has been long in preparation,) to be called

The ELFIN SPRITE,
AND
The Grim Grey Woman.

With new Scenery, Machinery, Dresses, and Decorations.
The principal Characters by Mr. KEELEY, Mr. W. H. PAYNE, Mr. HAINES, Mr. HENRY,
Mr. F. MATTHEWS, Mrs. VINING, Miss ROMER, Miss POOLE, Mrs KEELEY.

A programme dated 1833 announcing a tragedy, a farce and a ballet, all to be given on the same evening.

Introducing the theatre

own town. Find out when it was built, what architect designed it and what plays have been produced there. Perhaps famous players of the past acted there. What sort of lighting equipment is installed and where do they store the scenery?

If you are very polite and the theatre manager has some spare time and a kind nature, he may help you a great deal. You could include plans of stage and auditorium, printed programmes or old programmes you have copied down in the local library or museum, photographs, pieces of material, drawings, folding models and newspaper cuttings.

Alternatively you could make one particular well-known play your subject and try to find out about all the productions of it throughout the years. You could describe the theatre in some past age, follow the creation of a set of stage costumes from the first idea to the completed costume or make a project on stage lighting. Or take a famous actor or actress and trace his or her career from the very first small part onwards.

A good amateur company is not to be despised and an interesting project could be made from a play produced by you and your friends, as long as you did everything as well as you possibly could.

But I am sure you can think up projects for yourselves. If you have ever done any research you will know that, although it needs patience and perseverance, it can be as exciting as detective work. If you can once start the trail (perhaps in your local library, where the librarian will usually be very helpful, or perhaps by asking the right people the right questions) one clue leads to another till finally you have collected a surprising amount of information.

Note When referring to work in the theatre the pronoun 'he' has been used in this book for the sake of convenience. In fact, most stage jobs are equally open to men and women.

2 Plays and playwrights

Tragedies from ancient Greece to today

Shakespeare

Various kinds of comedies

Watching plays we do not understand

New fashions in play writing

Tragedy
Plays were once divided up into tragedies and comedies. A *tragedy* tells of sad or terrible events that lead up to an unhappy ending. In old times tragedies were usually about kings and queens or mythical heroes doomed to a terrible fate. All the characters spoke in poetic language.

Ancient and modern
The first tragedies we know of were written by the ancient Greeks nearly 2,500 years ago. Some of their plays are so wonderfully written that they can still move us deeply today although their world and their way of speaking are so different from ours. For example when Olivier played the part of King Oedipus in the play of that name by Sophocles, and it came to the part where he persists in trying to find out the secret of his birth, little knowing that the discovery will ruin him and all his family, the audience could hardly bear the suspense.

Many of our own playwrights in the reigns of Elizabeth I and James I wrote thrilling tragic plays. William Shakespeare, the greatest of them all, had such a wide feeling for life that he sometimes interrupted his tragedies with those funny moments that can happen even during sad events. He may have felt that they made the dark and terrible parts of the play seem even

Plays and playwrights

A portrait of William Shakespeare. The illustration is the famous Droeshout engraving, the frontispiece of the First Folio.

darker by contrast. He had a deep understanding of people's hearts and thoughts and his language is so lovely to hear and his choice of words so clever that his lines are not only exciting to listen to but also a joy for actors to speak. In fact, being an actor himself, he had a sense of the theatre, that is to say he knew what sounds and looks effective on the stage. Many great writers, including Tennyson and Browning, have failed when they tried to compose plays, because they had never learnt that secret.

Two of Shakespeare's greatest tragedies were *Hamlet* and *Macbeth*. See if you can find the titles of three more and when they were written.

Plays and playwrights

Later on in the seventeenth century some of these tragedies turned into plays of mere horror and revenge. Here and there they contain lovely lines of poetry, but in the last scene there are usually too many corpses lying about for us to take it quite seriously. Try to discover the names of these plays and their authors.

Some modern plays are tragic too, but they are usually more realistic than the old ones. A musical film called *West Side Story*, made a few years ago, was based on the plot of Shakespeare's tragedy *Romeo and Juliet*.

Comedies

A *comedy* is a light, amusing play with a happy ending. The characters speak and behave more like people in everyday life. The Greeks and Elizabethans wrote comedies too. Match up your three Shakespearean tragedies with three of his comedies. At the end of the seventeenth century, about fifty to seventy years after Shakespeare's death, there was a great mode for elegant comedies about fashionable people not very like real life. These had very complicated stories in which young ladies and gentlemen were constantly falling in and out of love with each other, while older ones were plotting all sorts of mischievous intrigues. The best of these comedy-writers was William Congreve. He was very witty and could invent the most delightful conversations — called 'dialogue' — in a play. One of his most famous comedies was called *The Way of the World.* It is still acted quite often.

Nearly a hundred years later Richard Sheridan wrote comedies. The four he wrote in the 1770s were witty and amusing too but more kindly and natural than Congreve's. There are sure to be some copies of his works at school or in the local library. Try dipping into *The Rivals* or *The School for Scandal* and see if you enjoy them.

The sort of comedy Sheridan and Congreve wrote is called a comedy of manners, because it makes fun of the way people talk and behave. A romantic comedy is, of course, chiefly about love and heroism and is not necessarily funny at all.

In the early years of this century the famous George Bernard Shaw was writing a new sort of comedy which was like an

Plays and playwrights

argument about politics and what people believed and the way the country was being run. He helped all this down with such amusing stories and brilliant talk that audiences listened enthralled and went home to argue some more. This type of play came to be called the comedy of ideas. Shaw died in 1950 aged ninety-four. Among his best-known plays were *Man and Superman* and *St. Joan*. I wonder if you can discover the name of a play of his that was turned into a tremendously successful musical a few years ago.

A comedy is not always meant to make you laugh aloud. A play that is written to keep you laughing all the time is called a farce. A farce is full of ridiculous mistakes with the characters running in and out of different doors and falling over and losing their

A portrait of George Bernard Shaw in 1906.

heads or their trousers. Shakespeare's *Comedy of Errors* was really more a farce than a comedy. It is about two sets of identical twins who keep getting mixed up. There is a famous farce called *Charley's Aunt* written in Queen Victoria's reign that still makes us laugh. It shows all the absurd things that happened when an Oxford student dressed up as his friend's aunt. Brian Rix is still acting in plays like that today.

Different ways of writing plays
In time playwrights began to find it more and more difficult to fit their plays into these neat compartments, and new divisions were invented such as tragi-comedy, melodrama, romantic drama and thriller. Then there are entertainments in which different arts are mixed together. What do we call a play in which the actors sing their parts instead of speaking them? Or an entertainment made up entirely of dancing to music? Next time you watch a television play or film decide what heading you would put it under.

Some plays are intended to be as like real life as possible in the way the characters behave and the world they live in. Such plays are called realistic. When this is overdone, so that everything on the stage is made to appear as real as possible — live sheep in the make-believe farmyard, ripe fruit on the table, solid doors and so on, the method is called naturalistic. There is nothing wrong with it when it is suitable, but there are many kinds of play it does not suit at all. Some plays seem quite unreal but have a real truth hidden in them, as in fantasies and symbolic plays. Plays are known as symbolic when the story or characters are symbols, that is, they stand for something else. For instance, there is a very old play called *Everyman* that shows a rich man at a feast with his friends Riches, Friendship and the rest. When a character in black called Death approaches they leave him one by one. Only newcomers such as Good Works and Repentance can help him then. But symbols are not always made as easy to understand as that.

We must not forget that an interested audience is always willing to use its imagination. It would rather imagine sheep that were not there in an interesting play than see real sheep in a boring one.

Plays and playwrights 11

How much do you consider an appearance of reality improves a play? When would it help most?
Perhaps you have sometimes felt deeply involved in a play — that is to say, so much inside it that you wanted to fall about with laughter or cry or cheer, or perhaps you have liked one character and hated another. Have you ever been moved almost to tears, not because something is sad but because it is so perfectly done? Or, in spite of its sadness, have you felt your spirit lifted up because there was something fine about it?
When a theatrical entertainment has that mysterious quality that appeals to something inside us we can enjoy it even when it is difficult to understand and not at all like real life.
Let us take an example. The Kathakali dancers of India look very strange to us. The men paint their faces green, have tall golden head-dresses and wear short crinoline skirts over white trousers. A narrator chants a story of the adventures of gods, goddesses, heroes and demons and then, in the light of flickering torches, the actors mime and dance it to the music of drums. It is difficult for a European to understand their gestures unless he has read the story beforehand — and yet he can watch them, fascinated, for hours.
The actors in ancient Greek tragedy were doing much the same thing except that they spoke. The chief characters wore masks and padded clothes to show they were more than human, but the audience knew the old stories and entered into all their feelings and misfortunes.

Experiment

There are some modern plays too that are fascinating to watch and listen to even when we are not too sure of their inner meaning, like the plays of Samuel Beckett or Harold Pinter. These are among the greatest modern playwrights and you might well refer to them and their plays in your project.
All through history people have made rules about how plays should be written and then new authors have come along and broken the rules. If there were no experiments there would be no discoveries. On the other hand a play needs some sort of form just as our bodies need a skeleton.
The present age is a time of rule-breaking and experiments in

Plays and playwrights

A Kathakali dancer from India.

Plays and playwrights

all the arts. Some of it will turn out to be valuable, while some is just silly fashion-following. For there are fashions in plays just as there are in clothes. Fashions come and go. Many plays appear, many are popular in their time, but only very, very few have that vital quality that makes them live on through the ages. It must not be forgotten that the British theatre is often influenced by theatre in other lands, just as those countries are sometimes influenced by ours. It would be interesting to add to your project as many names of foreign playwrights as you can find.

Do you know how a play looks on the printed page? What are stage directions? What does 'exit' mean?

Nothing teaches us as much as trying to do a thing ourselves. So, if you are interested in writing, you could try this exercise. Invent three or four characters (touchy old lady, inquisitive child, sensitive teenager, for example — only please invent your own) and place them in a special situation such as a bus journey or waiting at the gates of heaven. Think how each of these people would feel and speak, and write one or two pages of dialogue. Nothing very exciting need happen to them unless you want it to, but it must be lifelike.

3   Construction

About the various parts of a theatre building

Some differences between a theatre and a cinema

Planning so that everyone can see well

As soon as there is space for one or two actors and room for a few people to watch them you have some sort of theatre. There are certain acting companies that travel about the country in a van carrying a set of screens or curtains, a few theatrical costumes and a great deal of enthusiasm. They are prepared to present their plays in school halls, tents, parks or any other place where an audience is ready to welcome them. If you have seen a performance given by a company like that, you will know how good they can be.

A tour of the theatre
But I want to begin by describing a large professional theatre of the usual type. When we go to see a play we book our tickets at the box office, then go through a pleasant room called the foyer to the auditorium where we shall find our seats. Downstairs are the stalls, the most expensive places, and above them curve two or three balconies. The lowest is the dress circle with front seats costing as much as stalls, those further back being cheaper. Then comes the upper circle and, highest and cheapest of all, the gallery, now sometimes no longer in use. The gallery audience used to be known as the gods, perhaps because they were so high up and could decide whether the play was to be a success or not.
Long ago the lower balconies were divided into little rooms called boxes — hence the name box-office. Even now curtained boxes are often seen on either side of the stage. In opera houses,

Construction

Nottingham Playhouse, a modern theatre, opened in 1963.

which are grander than ordinary theatres, there are still boxes all round the front of the balconies.

The older theatres are often splendidly decorated with crimson velvet and golden wreaths or cupids. A dazzling chandelier hangs from the ceiling and the stage is concealed behind a rich curtain.

Years ago there were always musicians in the so-called orchestra pit just below the stage. To visit the theatre one put on one's best clothes and when the orchestra tuned up and then played till a light shone at the base of the curtain to show that it was about to rise, it all seemed very festive.

Now, more often than not, the curtain will already be up when you come in, showing the stage quite dark and empty, though you know it will soon be filled by light and players.

You may think that up to now I might as well have been describing a grand cinema. In fact there are very important differences between the two kinds of building, but, apart from the screen itself, they are mostly hidden from view.

Construction

The stage
The cinema has a shallow stage and there need not be much room behind or above it. In a theatre the area of stage we see from the auditorium is only a small part of the whole. The unseen space above it is more than as high again so that there is room for scenery such as backcloths to be hauled up there on ropes and hang there till wanted again. This is called 'flying' the scenery and because of that the space over the stage is called the 'flies'. It is surrounded by dizzily high galleries from which the scene-shifters can adjust and fasten the ropes. Still higher is the grid supporting all the lines and pulleys.

The stage itself is twice as wide as the part you see through the opening so that actors waiting to enter, pieces of scenery for the next act and lighting equipment can stand there out of sight. These side spaces are called 'wings'. (Can you think of any other people or objects that might have to stand hidden in the wings?) The stage also extends a long way behind the acting area.

In front of the stage there is a sort of frame – or at least the top and sides of a frame – known as the proscenium, or 'pros' for short. If it were not for the proscenium the audience might see more than they are meant to – the top edge of the backcloth, perhaps, or actors waiting in the wings.

To be sure that everyone in the audience gets a good view of the stage the architect planning a theatre, or a designer working out the size and placing of the scenery, has to be very careful about what are called sight-lines. He marks the place of the seats furthest to the side, nearest to the front and highest in the gallery. Using a scale plan and elevation (which is a vertical view) of the theatre he draws straight lines from those positions to the stage to make sure that everyone in the audience will not only see enough of the acting area but also does not see too far beyond it.

If you make a rough and ready sort of model stage with a frame round the front of it and try out these sight-lines by moving to different sides of the room, then sitting on the floor and standing up, you will soon see how the audience's view has to be blocked in some way.

One way of doing this is to have a white or pale blue plaster wall or curtain at the back of the stage curved into a shallow bow shape and, ideally, curving inwards at the top as well. It must not

Construction

Sight lines

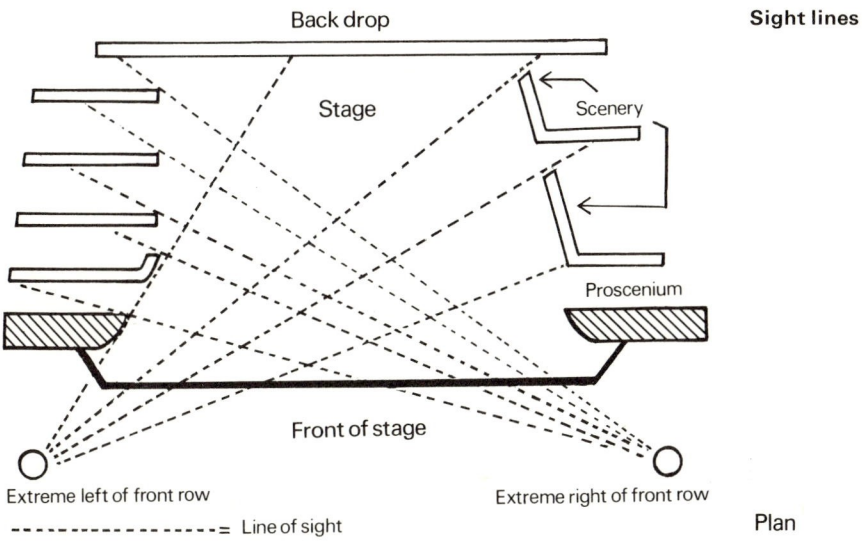

Plan

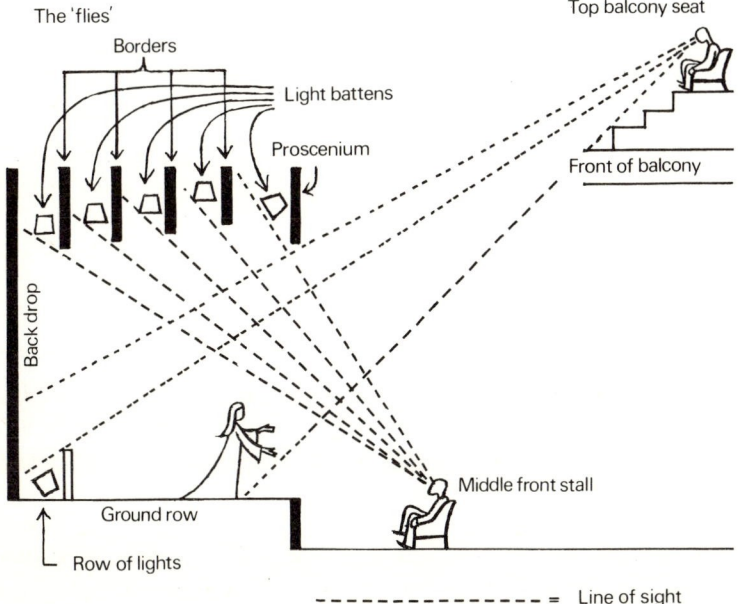

Elevation

be curved too far forward or it would get in the way of scenery and side entrances. This curved wall is called a cyclorama. It allows wonderful sky effects and is a better surface for lighting than an ordinary flat backcloth.

There are many other ways in which a theatre is different from a cinema. In the floor of the stage there are usually trap doors as well as platforms that can be raised up by machinery. Arranged somewhere near the stage are dressing-rooms, a room called the wardrobe, where costumes are kept and looked after, a scenery store, lighting cabin, workshops and various other rooms and offices.

In some theatres there is a room for the actors to meet in, known as the greenroom because in the old days the wallpaper in these rooms was green. The actors and stage staff go in and out of the building by a special door at the back or side. It is called the stage door and is guarded by the stage door keeper who, among other things, sees to it that unwanted people do not get inside. See if you can find out what the words 'rostrum' and 'props' mean in a theatre. What is a 'safety curtain' and what are the rules for its use? Who makes the rules and who makes regular inspections to see that they are carried out?

Examples of beautiful old London theatres designed in the way I have described are the Drury Lane and Haymarket Theatres and Covent Garden Opera House. The Theatre Royal in Bristol, a lovely little playhouse, was built in 1766. In some other towns there are other old theatres still in use. During the eighteenth century many theatres were burnt to the ground because gas and electric lighting had not yet been invented. The candles and lamps they had to use were highly dangerous.

Modern theatres

Although most existing theatres are of the pattern I have outlined above, when a new one is built the design is nearly always different. People want to try out new ideas or go back to shapes that were used in ancient times. If you have a camera it would be interesting to take photographs of the outsides of as many theatres as you can.

New plans usually involve doing away with the proscenium. Many of the new theatres have an 'open stage' like the London

Construction

'Mermaid', arena stages that jut far out so that the audience sits along three of its sides, or even a circular stage (theatre in the round) with the audience all round it as in a circus. With the last, of course, there can be no scenery in the usual sense. One remarkable theatre called the Minack was constructed in the 1930s on the slope of a Cornish cliff rising high above the Atlantic. It is in the form of a Greek amphitheatre. Rows of stone or grass seating curve round the cliff, looking down on a stage that has only sea and rocks as its backcloth.

An argument

Many people still think the 'picture-frame stage' is the best possible way to show a play. 'The stage seen through a proscenium', they say, 'gives a perfect illusion of reality. There is nothing to destroy that illusion, such as glimpses of scenery edges, ropes or anything outside the action. Seated in the dark with nothing to distract them, the audience can give their whole attention to the play.'

'We don't want an illusion', argues the other side. 'We don't

The arena of the Octagon Theatre, Bolton.

want to imitate surface reality. We are acting a play. The audience should not be separated from the actors as if they were in another world. They should all be part of the same thing. A stage at one end with everyone acting towards the front is artificial.'

'Unfortunately,' answer the first speakers, 'actors have faces only on one side of their heads. If half the auditorium were behind them the audience could not hear well or watch the actors' facial expressions. The players would have to spin about like tops.'

Which do you think is right? Both, perhaps? Well, some theatres are planned so that both stage and auditorium can be altered and thus change their shape according to the play. But then again these have been described as 'suitable for everything, good for nothing'.

The outside of theatres can now be made into shapes never used before because of the use of reinforced concrete. This means that the weight of the building is carried on a framework so that the balconies and other parts can jut out from the main building without any support beneath.

If you are the sort of person who enjoys planning and organizing, you could design your own ideal school theatre as if you had thousands of pounds to spend on it.

Those who have a real theatre in their neighbourhood should do their best to examine it. If not, take a look at the next best thing, such as a cinema or village hall, and think what you would like to do to improve it for the performance of plays.

Production   4

The director compared to the conductor of an orchestra

The work he has to do: thinking about the play and its meaning, about the audience, and about the actors

Rehearsals

If you have watched a symphony orchestra in a concert hall or on television you will have noticed the conductor standing in evening dress on a platform in front of the musicians, beating time with his baton. Sometimes he points it at one of them to indicate that it is time for that player to join in. He may raise his arms to tell them to play more loudly, or lower them as a quiet passage approaches. At the end a great burst of applause rises from the audience. He turns to face them and bows.

But the greater part of the conductor's work was done preparing for the concert during rehearsals and when he planned how the whole symphony was to sound and how each musician was to interpret his part of it.

In the theatre there is a man or woman who has precisely the same task except that it deals with a play instead of a piece of music. He or she, too, must transform the marks on a printed page into a live performance and deal with pitch (note), volume (loudness), tempo (pace) and stress (emphasis). This person is known as the director. There is some confusion about this title. We in England used to say 'producer' but now we have adopted the American term 'director'.

Before this century, however, no one had heard of either a stage producer or a stage director. A good deal of the work he does today was then undertaken by the stage manager, who is now a sort of second-in-command to the director. There were also leading actors who formed their own theatre companies and were called 'actor managers'. That was not always a good thing, firstly because the great actor could not take an outside view of the play since he was so often on the stage doing his part, and secondly because he tended to put his own part before any other consideration. There is a story about an old-time manager of this kind. When a new member joined the cast he would say 'There is only one rule in my company. Never stand between me and the audience!'

Some famous actor managers, however, such as David Garrick in the eighteenth century and Sir Henry Irving and Sir Johnston Forbes Robertson in the nineteenth, did great service to the theatre.

The director's job

The art of the theatre is made up of many different elements — writing, acting, design, lighting and so on. There has to be someone in overall control, trying to blend them into a unity. Without that the productions would be chaotic. The author knows more or less what effects he wants his play to have, but he seldom possesses enough stagecraft to know how that effect

Rehearsal for The Winter's Tale, *Royal Shakespeare Company, Stratford and London, 1969–70. Trevor Nunn (director) seated right. Standing: Lisa Harrow, David Bailie and John Broome; seated foreground: Judi Dench.*

Production

can be achieved. Can you think of other professions where this sort of overall control is necessary?

The director's work starts long before the time of rehearsals. A play has been chosen. He must read and re-read it and think about it a great deal. What sort of play is it? What is its general idea and feeling? What should it look like? He needs to ponder on all the characters to decide how they should be presented and why they say and do the things they do (motive).

Some people love acting but have no ambition to organize and direct plays. Many, however, feel that production is one of the most exciting jobs in the theatre. If you are one of them, I suggest that at this point you pick out a good one-act play or a scene from a play that appeals to you. Then you will have something definite to which you can relate the ideas and methods described in this chapter. Here are a few suggestions, though it would be better still to find your own play:

A scene from *Billy Liar* by Keith Waterhouse and Willis Hall. Act II of *Wild Decembers* by Clemence Dane (a play about the Brontë sisters).

Sir Henry Irving, the famous Victorian actor manager.

The Private Ear by Peter Schaffer.
Scenes from *RUR* or *The Insect Play* (science fiction and fantasy) by Karel Capek.
Riders to the Sea by J. M. Synge (a tragic one-act play).
A scene from *Charley's Aunt* by Brandon Thomas (a farce).

If a play were acted all on one note it would be very likely to send the audience into a deep sleep. The director must consider when the most important moment of the play is reached — the most exciting, the saddest, the most meaningful, or the funniest, according to the play. This high point is called the climax and often comes just before the end of an act. It must be worked up to. It must stand out, perhaps, by being louder or quieter, faster or slower than the rest, perhaps even by silence. There are lesser climaxes to be marked, and also lines that must be stressed in some way because they are key sentences in regard to character or plot. Next time you see a play, whether in theatre or cinema or on the television screen, try to spot the climax and other high points.

The director must follow the author's intention but have his own vision of how the play should be produced. He should be able to accept a suggestion and yet follow his own ideas when he feels it is right, for to try to please everyone is to please no one. There are practical as well as artistic matters to be dealt with. The amount of money available is a very important consideration. The production must be adapted to the stage it will occupy and to the audience it is aimed at.

The set (stage with scenery and furniture) must be arranged so that the actors can enter and exit at the right places and have room to play their scenes. The director discusses this with the designer so that the latter can begin work on plans, models and sketches for scenery and costumes. There may be sounds and music in the play and there will certainly be lighting to plan with the chief electrician or lighting expert.

Planning moves and grouping
A very important part of the preparation is to plan the positions, moves and grouping of the cast. Moves should not be made without a purpose. The actors must arrive on the right part of

Production

the stage at the right moment without appearing to have gone there merely to follow the stage directions. If they move about all the time it will be distracting. Staying in the same place throughout the act will give a monotonous effect. An actor must not stand in front of another so that the latter is hidden from the audience. That is called 'masking'. Two people talking confidentially must stand close together, not shout at each other across the room. A person addressing an important speech to others should not stand downstage with his back to the characters he is supposed to be talking to. See if you can find out the meaning of 'downstage' and 'upstage'. What does it mean if we call a *person* 'upstage'?

'Prompt side' and 'opposite prompt' (or O.P.) are also terms heard in the theatre. They arose because when the director faces the actors his right hand is their left, which can be rather confusing. Perhaps you can find out why the two sides of the stage were given these names and which side is which.

To go back to our moves — take a parting speech such as 'I am leaving. I have nothing more to say to you.' First try saying it all in the centre of the room, then walking to the door and going out. After that try speaking the line 'I am leaving' while you stand in the centre, then walk to the door in silence, look back and say 'I have nothing more to say to you' as you stand with your hand on the door-knob, ready to go out. You will notice that the effect is quite different.

When there are several characters on the stage at once they should be grouped in a way that is interesting to look at, not ranged in a straight line at equal distances from each other. Grouping can convey meaning too. For instance, if one character in a scene is an outsider defying several people who are against him, he might take up his position on one side of the stage while all the others stand close together on the other side. All this would be fun to try out with a group of friends.

Variety

The director has to remember that members of an audience will allow their thoughts to stray if he gives them a chance. He has to stop them thinking about tomorrow's dinner or the argument they had the day before, by keeping them continually interested.

Variety of pitch and tempo will help him there.

Another matter to be settled before rehearsals begin is casting, that is to say deciding which actor or actress would be most suitable for each part and then seeing if he or she can accept the engagement. When that has been arranged the director usually meets the whole cast to read the play, discuss it and consider how the various characters should be portrayed.

Imagine how you would cast your play from among members of your school. If you have a group of friends already interested in acting you could organize a play-reading. Each reader needs a book from which he can study the play a little in advance and read his part on the day itself. The drama section of your county library will have sets of books of a great many plays. Smaller parts could be copied out if necessary.

Directing the actors
It is not the job of the director to tell professional actors exactly what to do and how to speak every sentence. That would worry and constrict them so that they could not create any feeling or character themselves. He has to draw the best out of them, not try to force his ideas in. It is a matter of give and take, and his ideas, as well as those of the cast, may develop and change during rehearsals. A director needs patience and tact. He must not expect everything at once. Far more is achieved by encouragement than by fault-finding. The idea of a director continually flying into rages is very old-fashioned. However he might keep a short burst of rage up his sleeve for special occasions. His decision should be final and he must have the authority and courage to enforce it. See if you can decide which people in your school would make the best theatrical directors. As rehearsals progress he will have to take care that the performance does not get out of balance so that too much weight is given to the wrong part. Sometimes he must spur the actors on, occasionally hold them back. Gradually the characters will begin to grow real and the play will come alive.

In many cases rehearsals will have to start in a large room. It is important to practise on the stage as soon as possible because

Production

voice and movement will feel quite different in new surroundings. If you have acted in a school play I expect you will have noticed that yourself.

In the later stages the director has to check that scenery, scene changes, and lighting are all in order and give the cast plenty of time to get used to them. Can you think of any other matters he should see to?

At the final dress rehearsal everything is supposed to be — but often isn't — exactly as it will be at a public performance. At last the dreaded, exciting occasion of the First Night arrives. After that the director's responsibility is over and he leaves it to the stage manager to see that the production does not go downhill during the run. Directors have become very important in the modern theatre.

Productions of well-known plays are often given in an unexpected form in order to throw fresh light on them and to suit the audience of today. The characters are depicted in a new way, eccentric stage 'business' may be introduced or the sets may all be made of transparent plastic, or the costumes suggest quite a different period from that of the play. Some people think that direction has become *too* important and that there are modern productions in which the author's intentions have been distorted by the director's gimmicks. This reminds me of the teasing comment made by Noel Coward, the famous actor and playwright. 'What producers are for', he said, 'is to stop the actors bumping into each other.'

5 Acting

The qualities an actor needs

Learning to act; practising a part; getting a job

Different kinds of actors

Stars

Do you know the story of the man who was asked if he could play the violin? 'I don't know,' he replied, 'I've never tried.' Sometimes people talk like that about acting. They think that if you have talent you may be 'discovered' the first time you set your foot on the stage!

In reality you might be bursting with feeling and thought about your part, but unless you had studied and practised you could not project it — that is to say, convey it to the audience. In the same way a gifted pianist has to play scales and exercises for years before venturing to play at a public concert and a great footballer has to train and practise every day for a long time before he is fit for a first division team. You can probably think of other examples.

A dramatic performance needs four qualities: (1) feeling, which includes imagination and emotion; (2) intelligence for understanding the play and the part; (3) a sense of character to make the actor real and living in that part; (4) technique, which means a knowledge of his craft and how best to use the instruments of his art. In what order of importance would you put these qualities?

A violinist's instruments are his hands, his violin and his bow, a painter's are his colours and brushes. An actor's tools are his voice and his whole body.

To appear natural on the stage it is not enough to behave just as you would in everyday life. You have to be understood by an

Acting 29

audience some of whom may be a long way from you, and so your voice and gestures have to be larger than life in order to seem natural.

Training to be an actor
The quickest and most thorough way to learn the skills of an actor (I include actresses in that word) is to study for two or three years at a drama school. After that the actor will still need the experience of acting in front of the public for some years, and, in fact, can go on improving throughout life.
Let us suppose you are a new student. As with singing, one of the first things to learn is correct breathing. The teacher puts her hand on your diaphragm (the muscle just below your breastbone) and says 'Breathe in deeply through your nose. No, no, not into the top of your chest like a pouter pigeon!' You try again. 'It's no good pushing your tummy out', she says this time. 'Keep it in and feel your breath expand your lower ribs. That's better. Hold it. Now let it out slowly through your mouth.'
Next time you are in a public place, such as a bus, notice people's voices. Far too many people speak in thin nasal tones as if breath in their lungs had nothing to do with it. Others slur their consonants (b, t, r etc.) or use narrow, twisted vowel sounds. In a theatre such voices would sound flat, difficult to hear and certainly not attractive. Even in ordinary life it is a pity to speak our wonderful, rich English language sloppily. The French take much more pride in theirs and cannot bear to hear it badly spoken.
And so our student goes on to diction exercises such as calling out the vowel sounds 'Ah – ee – ay – oh – oo', breathing correctly and using the palate just below the nose as a sounding board for resonance, or else hitting the consonants in p, b, n, t, hard and clear. Try these breathing and diction exercises yourself. What expression there can be in a single word! 'No', for instance, can be said decidedly, crossly, hesitantly, regretfully, teasingly or as a question. See if you can make 'no' express those meanings.
Movement on the stage is as important as speech. For a beginner it is strangely difficult at first to stand still on a stage or walk across it naturally or follow quite simple directions. That is

Sir Laurence Olivier in Oedipus Rex, *1946*

largely because he is tense and self-conscious. One of the first things taught is to relax. Here is a relaxation exercise. Stand very upright, every muscle tensed, then bit by bit relax head, neck, shoulders, arms, hands, spine, legs. Now you are bending loosely towards the floor. Before you actually collapse on to it, however, you gradually tense up and rise again.

There are fencing and dancing lessons to make the student nimble and graceful. He learns to use large, clear-cut gestures, not to make them unless they are necessary, and to stand still. A favourite training method these days is improvisation. Perhaps you do that in drama at school. Without preparation the class is given a simple incident or situation to act. They follow their own ideas but every action and object must be imagined in a very real way.

Among the things an actor has to be able to do naturally are laughing, crying, falling down and speaking in a whisper that

Acting

Sir Laurence Olivier as Othello at the National Theatre, 1967, directed by John Dexter, designs by Jocelyn Herbert.

can be heard all over the auditorium. Laughing and crying can both be done by breath control. Start by breathing out almost entirely, let out the last remnants of breath in little jerks, then take a great gasp of air in through your mouth. You can turn it into laughter or weeping according to how you have made yourself feel. This method avoids those sudden ha-has that sound so unconvincing in beginners. Experiment with this if you can find a private enough place!

The attention of the audience must be held not only by your sincerity but by variety of pitch, speed and volume. Gradually one acquires a sense of timing so that one knows when to hurry and when to pause, when to stress a line and when to throw it away, as it is called, and how much time to allow for the audience's laughter after a funny line. It would be very interesting to try speaking parts of plays into a tape recorder with your friends.

Acting and feeling

I do not want to give the impression that acting is a mere collection of tricks; but once you are armed with this technical knowledge you can express your feeling and imagination with full effect. Technique sets you free.

Acting put on from outside does not ring true. It has to start inside you. Although you may have spoken the line a hundred times it must sound each time as if it had just occurred to you for the first time a split second before you say it. The actor uses a double personality. One half *is* the person he portrays and feels his emotions, the other half is in control and knows he is in a theatre.

There is a story that when the great actress, Dame Edith Evans, was playing Millament in Congreve's *Way of the World* years ago she was quite unnecessarily nervous that the audience might not think her young and lovely enough for the part. So in her dressing-room before every performance she would murmur 'I am beautiful, I am beautiful' until the acting half of her was sure of it. When she swept on to the stage she looked so enchanting that the audience could hardly spare a glance for the other pretty and younger actresses!

When the actor's part is first handed to him he must read it over many times, thinking out what the character is like and the reasons for his words and deeds till he knows all about him and what he would feel. How would such a person hold his head, for instance? How would he walk? Try walking in different ways yourself, stealthily, shyly, miserably, happily, conceitedly, like an old man. What sort of voice would he have? Does the character change and develop during the play because of what happens to him? Where does the climax of the part come? Something must be kept in reserve for that. Select a character from your play and think about him or her in this way.

The actor must remember that he is seldom alone on the stage, however. He has to connect his part with the others, and watch or listen to the other players when he is silent. He may not drop out of his part just because he is not speaking. Next time you watch a play observe the non-speakers. It is not an easy thing to do if the play is interesting!

Not all stage parts are long and full of feeling, but small parts can be well done too. Supposing the part is that of a waiter with

Acting 33

very few words to speak, the careful actor will go to a restaurant and watch how a waiter carries plates, offers a dish or notes down an order. The small-part character must seem quite real, but it must be kept unobtrusive so that it does not distract attention away from the chief actors. Observe the playing of small parts too. What is an understudy?

Noel Coward tells an amusing story against himself. As a boy actor he came to audition for the part of a page in a play with the great comedy actor Charles Hawtrey (not the present one). He only had to make a simple announcement such as 'A gentleman left a letter, Sir. He's waiting for an answer.' He had been so carefully coached to say each word with beautiful diction and expression that it sounded like a grand speech. Hawtrey turned wearily to his stage manager, 'Tarver,' he said, 'never let me see that boy again!' In fact, he relented and Coward got the part on condition that he spoke like an ordinary page boy.

To speak Shakespeare well is something of a balancing act. The lines must sound real and alive and yet not lose their poetry. The rhythm must not tempt the actor to fall into sing-song intonations or enjoy the sound of his own voice at the expense of the meaning.

Looking for work

When the student leaves drama school the next problem is to find a job. On hearing that a production is being planned he or she will write for an audition. There are theatrical agents who will try to find acting work in return for about 10 per cent of the salary paid. Unfortunately there are more applicants than parts and many unemployed actors are to be found working in shops and restaurants on the understanding that they may leave quickly if a theatre job turns up.

On the first page of this book I said that working in the theatre could mean a hard life with poor pay. But there was a time when the life could be harder and the pay poorer than it is today. Top actors were able to make their own terms because the public demanded to see them, but ordinary members of the profession often had to tour from place to place in very uncomfortable conditions for tiny salaries.

Sometimes, if a play were not making enough money, the

manager would disappear with the takings from the box office, leaving the company stranded, penniless and far from home — and there was nothing they could do about it.

If a player complained about pay or conditions he might be dismissed. And he was afraid he would not get another job. Actors began to realize that they could only get reforms if they banded together into a sort of trade union, and so Actors' Equity was formed in 1930. Since then minimum salaries have been fixed. No professional actor may be paid less. There is also a standard contract — that is to say an agreement between actor and management, in which certain fixed conditions are laid down about pay, the number of performances to be given, and so on. No one may work as a professional actor unless he is a member of Equity, and he may not become a member unless he has worked for some time as an actor. That sounds as if it would be impossible to join — and indeed the Government as well as Equity *want* it to be difficult because there is so much unemployment in the theatre. But of course it is not impossible or there would never be any new actors. The beginner must join as a provisional member — like being a learner driver — then he may play small parts anywhere outside the West End, and when he has worked for a total of forty weeks he may apply for full membership.

Acting to an audience

What is needed after leaving drama school is the experience of playing the same part for a number of performances to gain confidence, and of acting in front of the public to learn the feel of an audience. No two audiences are ever quite the same. As Dame Edith Evans said 'You know by the way the lines are going whether they want a little gingering up or calming down!' Players and audience affect each other.

After the audition, three or more weeks of rehearsing and the ordeal of the first night there is one more occasion that the actor awaits in some suspense — reading the reviews of the play that appear in the newspapers. Did the critic like the play? Is your own name mentioned? Did he think you were good — or terrible? Even unfavourable criticism is not always destructive.

Acting

Vanessa Redgrave in the stage version of The Prime of Miss Jean Brodie *by Muriel Spark and J. P. Allen.*

Maggie Smith and Robert Stephens in the film version of The Prime of Miss Jean Brodie

It can be helpful, pointing out how, in the critic's opinion at least, play and playing could be improved.

If you read some dramatic criticisms in newspapers you will see how the critic puts his point of view and you could then write one yourself about the next play you see on television or elsewhere. Reviews of some performances you have seen will be an important part of your project.

Repertory theatres are the best training ground at this stage. During a repertory season a number of plays — four or five perhaps — are acted by the same company on different days of the week and month. The Old Vic and Stratford Memorial Theatre are the most famous playhouses of this type but there are a number of others. Can you discover where some of them are? The name, often shortened to 'rep', is also used for theatres where a company of actors performs a play for two or three weeks only and then changes to another. The work is hard because the players are often studying one part, rehearsing another and acting a third all in the same week. Is there a 'rep' theatre near your home?

Actors can also find employment in films, television and radio. Here, too, training for the stage is invaluable, but the actor will have to adapt his methods for these different kinds of acting. Voice and gesture must be quieter and smaller. Emphasis, pauses, changes in pitch and volume will all appear exaggerated. Hence the playing will have to be more subtle. A tiny eye movement that would be invisible in a theatre can mean a lot in close-up. Insincerity and showing off are shown up without mercy.

In film-making the scenes are taken in short sessions with long waits between. They are not always in the right order of the story and there is no audience to play to. A stage actor often finds it difficult to get into a film part at first.

And in radio, of course, everything has to be expressed by the voice alone.

Actors and actresses

There are two sorts of actor. The first kind always plays more or less the same kind of person, he plays himself. That is not quite as easy as it sounds. He projects a special type, often with great

Acting

skill. Probably you often turn on television or go to a film because you like to see so-and-so doing his usual sort of part.

The second kind — and this is more truly acting — changes himself with every part he plays. His voice, his walk, his mannerisms, his appearance are those of the character and not himself. An excellent example of this is the brilliant actor, Sir Alec Guinness. In a film called *Kind Hearts and Coronets* he once played eight separate parts, including two women, all quite different.

A few actors and actresses are of both these types. They change themselves to suit each role, but their own stage personalities are so strong that they shine through. I would put Sir Laurence Olivier and Dame Edith Evans in this class. See if you can think of other examples of the three types.

Some companies of actors play together like a football team, combining their efforts and, so to speak, passing the ball from one to the other, not trying to keep it to themselves all the time.

Sybil Thorndike as Joan of Arc in Bernard Shaw's St Joan, *1924.*

This is a healthy state of affairs for the theatre and to work in that sort of company is a joy. It is also splendid training.

Although the members of the National Theatre Company are all experienced actors, there are classes and instructors there to help them. When one of the leading actors, Robert Stephens, was chosen to play the Inca emperor in *The Royal Hunt of the Sun* by Peter Schaffer, he was not too proud to take speech lessons to get the right sort of voice and to attend gymnastic classes to develop muscles in just the right places.

In contrast to this kind of company there is the star system. Here the star player is considered more important than the play or the acting as a whole. In many ways this is a pity, but when the star has genius, that indescribable electric vitality, it is something worth going a long way to see, something to remember all one's life. Which system do you prefer?

Among the great actors in Britain today, besides those I have already mentioned, are Sir John Gielgud and Dame Sybil Thorndike. See if you can find the names of two other actors and two other actresses who have been made knights or dames for their services to the theatre.

You may say that none of these is young. That is because they have had time to learn their art and become famous. Of a younger generation there are the very talented Eric Porter, the lovely Vanessa Redgrave, that fascinating comedy actress Maggie Smith and many others.

As to the best of the newest batch of actors, it is for you to discover them for yourself. See if you can recognize the stars of the future. Be a talent spotter!

Design 6

The look of a play is of great importance

Different kinds of scenery and how they are changed

The work of the stage designer

How to find out about historical costume

What is the purpose of scenic and costume design in the theatre apart from looking beautiful? It must suit the play and characters so perfectly that it forms a part of them and adds to their effect even if we are not consciously aware of it. It creates atmosphere just as music can. The memory of the play that you carry home with you is inseparably mixed up with its appearance. Can you remember the general look of a play you have seen? A good design focuses attention where it is wanted. Sets or dresses that distract are bad design.
Scenery and costumes should ideally be planned by the same person for they form a unity. A set without actors is incomplete. If set and costumes are designed by two different people they must work closely together.

The 'set'
Occasionally plays are acted in front of curtains (known as 'tabs', short for *tableaux*, which is the French word for pictures). Otherwise, unless there is a cyclorama, a smooth canvas background known as a backdrop or backcloth is used. Most other scenery is made of canvas stretched over a framework of wood. The separate units are called 'flats'. They measure between 30 cm (1 ft) and 2 m (6 ft) or even 2.75 m (8 ft) wide and are as high as need be for the particular stage (sometimes as much as 8 m (24 ft)). They can be joined together at an angle or as one large surface. See if you can find out what 'wing-flats' are, and 'borders' and 'ground-rows'.

A wooden platform, foldable for storage, is a very useful piece of equipment for a stage. It is called a rostrum. Different levels make a set look interesting.

A room scene with three walls — the audience takes the place of the fourth — is called a box-set. Attached to it is a slanting ceiling that folds back when the scene is hauled up into the flies. See if you can find out the meanings of the following theatrical terms: boat-trucks, tormentors, flippers, set-piece, carpet cut. There are numerous practical points to be considered. The entrance and exits must be placed where they are needed and there must be enough room for the action. The lighting must be able to reach the right areas.

If there are scene changes the scenery has to be easy to set and strike (put in place and take away). Long waits can kill the audience's interest. One way to avoid delay is to use a revolving stage — that is a large circular insertion that can go round. It can hold two sets back to back (see illustration). First scene A is visible. Then it revolves to show scene B. Another quick way to change scenes is to play scene A in front of a backdrop near the front of the stage while a second, deeper set is being arranged behind it. The first backdrop then rises to reveal scene B. (If you are good at carpentry, or know someone who is, you can try these ideas out on a model stage made out of a platform supporting a simple framework of straight sticks.)

Scene changes can be avoided altogether by dividing the stage into several different areas representing, say, a bedroom, a living-room and a part of the garden, all seen at once.

Then there are permanent sets that do not have to be changed at all during the play and are often made up of adaptable units such as steps, pillars and arches. These have a solid three-dimensional look that is good for light and shadow. Scenes, still or moving, can be thrown on to the backcloth by an effects projector.

Planning a play's appearance

Before designing begins there must be a conference with the director. Sometimes he has a very definite idea of how he wants the production to look; more often he has only a vague notion.

Design

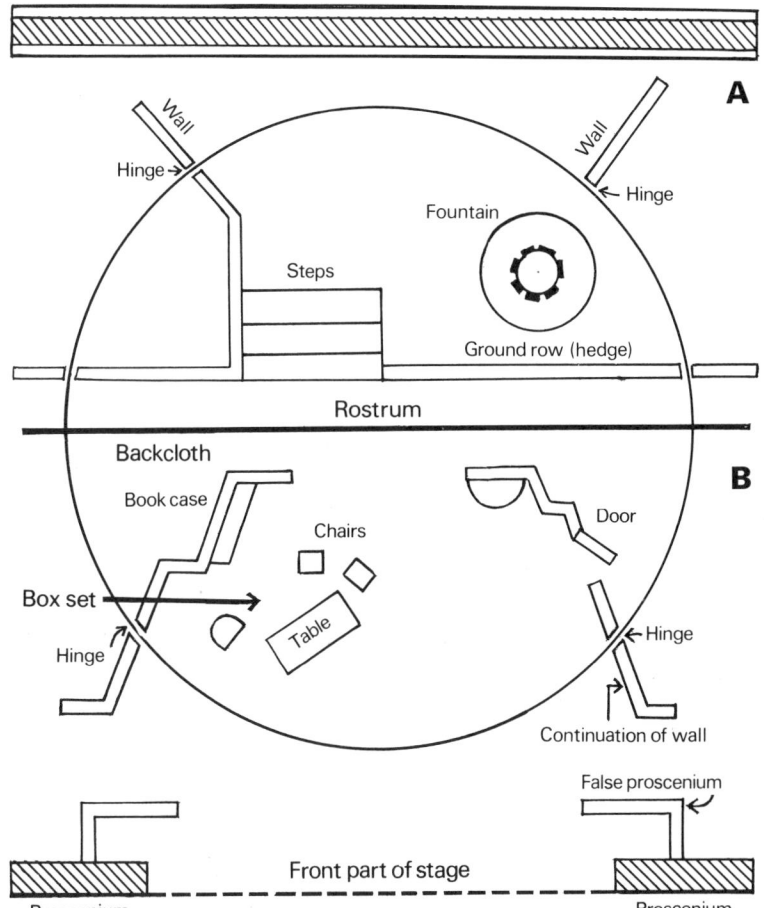

Revolving stage, showing scenes A and B.

In either case it is a long way from the first idea to the finished product.

Much thought must be spent on the play and its characters. The general style depends upon that. What is the prevailing mood? Is it grim, gay, realistic or fantastic? What is the period? Occasionally a play is set deliberately in a period other than its own. Shakespeare's *Hamlet*, for instance, has been played in modern dress. The idea behind that was to make the audience see it in a new light, not as a historical drama but as a play relating to our own time.

Sometimes the overall image springs into the designer's mind

Design

Costume design by Roger Furse for Sir Ralph Richardson as Falstaff.

almost at once, at others it remains blank for a while until suddenly some phrase or object — it could be the colour in a church window — provides the key, and the whole jig-saw puzzle falls into place.

Research is the next step. The designer must become familiar with the reality you are going to turn into theatrical illusion. He may have to inspect a Lancashire cotton factory, a doctor's waiting-room, a ducal drawing-room or a lakeland landscape. It is surprising how unobservant we all are until we really look. Try drawing without a model something fairly familiar, a car or a cow perhaps, and you will see what I mean. If you cannot examine the actual subject you will have to depend on photographs or pictures.

Costume

With historical costumes the designer must steep himself in the period, sketching interesting dresses and details from clothes in museums, paintings and books, finding where possible patterns of how the garments were cut. It is better to work from pictures made at the time than from modern books on historical

Design 43

Set design by Roger Furse for Macbeth, *Old Vic Company, 1955.*

costume because the former convey a truer sense of the period. For dates after 1850 there is nothing like old copies of *Punch* because they show people dressed in their everyday clothes, not got up in their best silks and jewellery for a portrait. You might find it interesting to visit your nearest picture gallery or museum to make notes or sketches of costumes or hair-dos you particularly like.

The general outline is the first point to watch. Next to that comes hair style. How often a correct costume is quite spoilt by modern-looking hair! Then one must observe materials, favourite patterns, necklines, waists, corsets, shoes etc. Think of other features to be noted. See if you can design a stage costume for a lady-in-waiting at the court of Charles I or for an Indian god. If you like dressmaking it would be fun to make a historically correct costume for a doll. But remember that exact copies, even genuine and antique clothes are not effective in the theatre. Reality has to be slightly exaggerated, simplified or reduced to its essence. Your research should be like using a dictionary to find words to compose a poem.

When a painter makes a picture he has to find the right balance of mass and line (composition) and the right balance of colours.

A simple model stage.

The stage designer has the same task, but in his case the picture moves. The human figures come and go, arrange themselves in varying groups, change their clothes or appear in front of different backgrounds. Often it is important for one character to stand out from the rest. A colour scheme needs careful thought. Could you design costumes and a set for a play about the Sleeping Beauty?

Seeing the job through

After the necessary research the designer probably begins by scribbling quantities of rough sketches, then goes on to finished drawings and ground plans, elevations and models to scale (usually 1.25 cm ($\frac{1}{2}$ inch) to 30 cm (1 ft)). All these must be passed by the director.

The next step is to explain your sets to the scene-builders and painters, who sometimes work in the theatre but more often at an outside scene-painting studio.

Costumiers must be consulted. In important theatrical productions the clothes are usually specially designed, but there are

Design

Perspective scenery in the late 17th century. The actual stage area does not go as far back as appears. Beyond the fourth pillar there is a painted backdrop to carry on the illusion.

times when they have to be hired. It is also important that the actors should feel happy in their costumes. The right costume is a great help.

The designer must also select materials, watch the progress of scene-painting, attend costume fittings and be present at some rehearsals, especially the final lighting, set, costume rehearsals and dress rehearsals (the last two are not one and the same occasion). It is very exciting for a designer to see the curtain go up on the final result of his early imaginings.

A stage designer needs an art-school training. It is also desirable to have practical experience of scene painting and costume making. He or she has to be interested in history, art history, literature and architecture.

7 Lighting and other jobs in the theatre

How stage lighting works; floodlights, spotlights, house lights

Colour in stage lighting

The work of the stage manager

Carpenters, scene-painters, wardrobe mistresses, dressers and others

Why do we light up a stage? 'To see what is going on there' seems the obvious answer. Yes, but there is a great deal more to it than that. The lighting expert has to be something between an artist and a scientist.

Lighting equipment
If you can get permission to look behind the scenes in a theatre you will find, high up behind the proscenium or at the side of the stage, a large electrical switchboard holding a great number of handles and switches. (Perhaps your school stage has one.) They are connected to several different kinds of lighting equipment in various parts of the theatre. Over the stage, hidden by proscenium or borders, hang one or more rows of light bulbs fastened to long beams. These are called battens (batten no. 1 at the front, no. 2 further back and so on). Similar lines of lamps may be laid behind ground-rows or attached to upright posts in the 'wings', when they are called 'strips'. The well known name 'footlights' (or 'floats') was given to a line of lamps running along the floor in a sort of trench at the front of the stage, but they are seldom seen nowadays. In their place we use front-of-house (F.O.H.) lighting, which comes from spotlights arranged on the front of the dress circle or balcony and aimed at the stage. Notice them next time you go to a theatre. The lighting in the windows of a big store can be interesting too. Other

Lighting and other jobs in the theatre

floodlights and spotlights stand in the wings or hang above the stage. The angle of light is important. (Can you find out the difference between 'floods' and 'spots', or what is illuminated by 'house lights'?)

These sources of light can be used together or separately. They can be turned on and off at once, or be made to 'come up' or 'dim' very gradually. It is the acting areas and, above all, the actors' faces that must be illuminated.

Shade is necessary as well as light. If there is equal lighting coming from all directions the stage picture tends to look uninteresting and it is difficult to see facial expression.

Compare this with the lighting of an ordinary room. One bare electric bulb hung from the centre of the ceiling will enable you to see your way around. If, however, you can manage to illuminate the room with wall-lights, shaded lamps or concealed lighting in an alcove, it will look much more attractive.

On the other hand, a carelessly placed floodlight could throw an actor's shadow on to a backcloth representing the sky, while a light coming from one direction only could cast a very unbecoming shadow on his face. If you have no model theatre try stretching a square of white material over an empty frame, stand it upright and place one or two small objects in front. Then you can experiment with the aid of two or three electric torches.

What can be done with colour

The rows of electric lights already mentioned — battens, strips and footlights — consist of different coloured bulbs, usually white, amber, green, red and blue in recurring order.

To give the impression of glowing summer all the amber and some of the red could be turned on, but only very few of the blue and white. A predominance of blue, white and green would suggest a cold winter dawn. If necessary the lights can be changed during the course of a scene. For instance, a golden afternoon could turn to sunset and then dusk.

All sorts of coloured or 'frosted' slides called gelatines can be inserted in front of the floods and spotlights.

You have probably used and discussed the primary colours in your art class. They are colours which cannot be obtained by

Lighting and other jobs in the theatre

Stage with lighting equipment.

mixing others, but which will produce various new colours when mixed together. You know that blue and yellow, primary colours, mixed together will make green, a secondary colour.

The primary colours of light, however, are different. They are red, blue and *green*. Red and blue light still combine to make purple, but red mixed with green will become *yellow*! Can you discover what colour results when all three primaries are mixed? Try mixing the same colours from your paint box and you will get a very different result.

If you have made the light-testing equipment suggested above, get some coloured glass or cellophane. Put it over the torchlights, try some of the ideas below, and invent more of your own. Light an object on your 'stage' with beams of 'complementary' (in this case opposite) colours, one pure primary on one side and a mixture of the other two primaries from the other. An example: purple (red + blue) from the left will naturally make the object look purple on its left surface, while a green light from the right side will make its right side green. Where the two beams meet, however, the light will be white.

Lighting and other jobs in the theatre

Coloured light can have unexpected results on coloured materials. Both the lighting expert and the scenic and costume designer have to be aware of that.
A red light cast on to blueish green makes it look black. Shine a red light on a scarlet figure in front of a white background and it practically disappears. Then see what happens when you throw a blue-green light on to the same scene.

Special effects
If you replace your plain white 'backcloth' by one made of some thin, gauzy fabric painted with a scene or pattern in aniline dye or water colour, you will get different effects according to whether you light it entirely from in front or from behind only. By the same means, an object placed behind the gauze can be made to appear and disappear.
Stage lighting can be used to suggest an atmosphere — the sun-dappled peace of a forest glade, the splendour of a princely ballroom or the gloom of a prison cell. In a realistic play the light must be accounted for in some way, so that it appears to come from say a window, a chandelier or the moon (think of other possible sources of light), although, in reality, it may be falling from several other directions. This is called 'motivated' light.
Bright light can focus your attention on one part of the stage, leaving the rest dark, perhaps for another scene later on.
The complicated lighting equipment of a full-size theatre can produce truly wonderful effects. The chart telling the electrician exactly which lights to use and when to change them is called the 'lighting plot' and is a very long and detailed document. However, a great deal can be achieved with much simpler equipment.
Take some real or imaginary play and imagine a scene from it that requires a rather special atmosphere and some change in lighting. Think of how you would light it and then write a simple lighting plot that would remind you how to set your lights at the beginning and when to change them.
The position of chief electrician in a big production is a very responsible one requiring much skill and experience.

Lighting and other jobs in the theatre

Stage management and other jobs

The stage manager is the person who has to ensure that the whole production and all its parts are staged exactly as planned. He is at the director's side while it is being rehearsed, he can take a rehearsal if the director is absent and he organizes everything connected with the stage. After the first night is over he has to see that the production keeps up to standard.

There is usually only one assistant stage manager; he is known as the A.S.M. or general dogsbody, and is often a budding actor or actress. A big theatre like the National, however, has a bewildering list of directors, managers and assistants to supervise the various departments.

If there is a scenic department in the building there will be skilled carpenters and scene-painters.

The designer's picture of the set is 'squared off' so that it can be copied by the painter square by square on a much larger scale – usually twenty-four times larger. To understand how this works, rule regular rows of perfect squares, on a small picture. Then, on a sheet of paper, draw a 'frame' four times longer and wider than the original. Fill it with the same arrangement of squares also four times bigger. Now it will not be difficult to make an enlarged copy by transferring the lines of the drawing from each small square to each large one. You cannot be a scene-painter, however, without a good knowledge of painting.

The wardrobe mistress has charge of all costumes, repairing, cleaning and altering them when necessary.

Leading actors and actresses usually employ dressers – who have often been with them for years – to assist them with quick costume changes and help generally in the dressing room.

The property master – but I remember that in Chapter 3 I asked you to find out about 'props' for yourself.

There are also assistant electricians, brawny scene-shifters and a host of others who all contribute their part to the production and mostly feel a justified pride in their craft.

If I have not mentioned musicians it is because the musical side of the theatre – including opera, ballet and musicals – is a subject needing a whole book to itself.

History of the British theatre 8

Early influences: primitive religious theatre; the ancient Greeks

Plays in the churches; plays in the streets; mystery plays

The first theatre building in England

Elizabethan playhouses; Court masques; Puritans and the theatre

New kinds of theatre after 1660

Some very famous actors

In this chapter we have time only to skim over the ocean of theatrical history, merely touching down here and there. If you are thinking of compiling a project about the theatre's past it may help you to decide which period interests you most.
Strangely enough it seems as if the theatre has nearly always sprung from religion. To this day there are primitive tribes in remote corners of the world who perform ceremonial dances as they pray for a good harvest and chant the praises and legends of their gods. A witchdoctor wearing a fearsome mask may sing the story, the dancers responding in chorus.
It was in just this way that the wonderful theatre in ancient Greece first arose — singer, mask, chorus, dancing and all. Its influence on our own theatre has been very great and many of our theatrical terms came from the ancient Greek theatre. See if you can trace the origin of our words 'scene', 'proscenium' and 'orchestra'.
The Romans took over the Greek theatrical traditions, but were rather too fond of extravagant display. In one production of the play *Clytemnestra* the treasure of Agamemnon was brought in on five hundred mules, and there were elephants and giraffes in the scene as well.

History of the British theatre

The theatre dies and is reborn
After the fall of Rome the only remnants of theatre left in Europe were wandering minstrels and jugglers. For a long time conditions in Europe were too unsettled for a real theatre to develop. Then once again, 1,500 years after the golden age of Greece, European drama was reborn out of religion. Simple representations of bible stories were enacted in the churches to help the many people who could not read to understand the gospels better.

Before long these plays became very popular and began to include comic episodes, so that in 1210 the Pope drove them out of the churches and into the towns, where they were usually organized and paid for by the trade guilds. Find out what the York and Coventry cycles were.

There were no regular theatres. Platforms on trestles were set up, sometimes backed by a tent, in town squares, so that people could move on from one to the other to see the various scenes or 'mansions' as they were called. The first often showed Adam and Eve in the garden of Eden, while the central position was kept for the Kingdom of Heaven where God the Father sat enthroned with the saints and angels on his right hand. I am afraid the scene on his left hand was more popular, however. This consisted of the mouth of Hell, often a fearsome dragon's head. Flames and smoke issued from its mouth at intervals while demons and monsters could be seen chasing the wicked with pitchforks. Other characters who surprisingly came to be considered comic were Herod, famous for getting into rages, Cain, and Noah's wife. To play the bigger scenes the actors usually descended into part of the square.

When there was no suitable large space in the city, the stages might be mounted on wheels. In that case the audience could stay on the same spot while the wagons (sometimes known as 'pageants' or 'triumphs') with their different scenes came round to them in turn.

In some parts of the country the people constructed circular acting places surrounded by earth walls just outside the town. Here temporary stages could be set up when wanted. There are two 'rounds' of this sort still remaining in Cornwall (can you find out where they are?) and of late years the old plays have been re-enacted there.

History of the British theatre

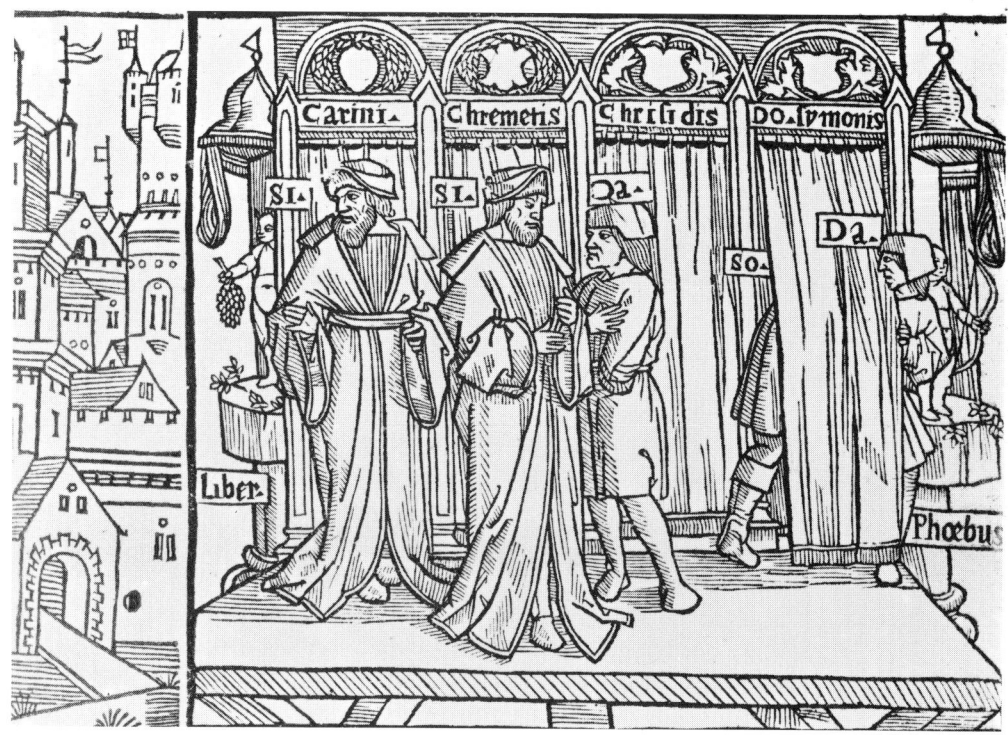

A street stage in the late Middle Ages. Woodcut from an early sixteenth-century French book of plays by Terence.

Though many of the 'mysteries', as these plays were called, are very simple, some have great charm and are not without humour. There is one about sheep-stealing Mak and the shepherds that turns in a moment from farce to devotion. See if you can trace it.

Not long ago a company of American singers toured the cathedrals of Britain performing *The Play of Daniel*, a French religious play of this time, just as it was written down. The words were all musically chanted. There were splendid costumes and plenty of dramatic action and it was altogether an enthralling entertainment.

In later mystery plays the clothes were often very costly and there was a great fondness for trick effects and 'machines'. Angels descended from Heaven, Hell's mouth gaped, Moses' staff burst into flower and when Judas was stabbed the entrails of a pig burst out of a bag concealed in his clothes, while a crow, representing his black soul, flew upwards.

Most of our knowledge of the Mysteries is derived from old

History of the British theatre

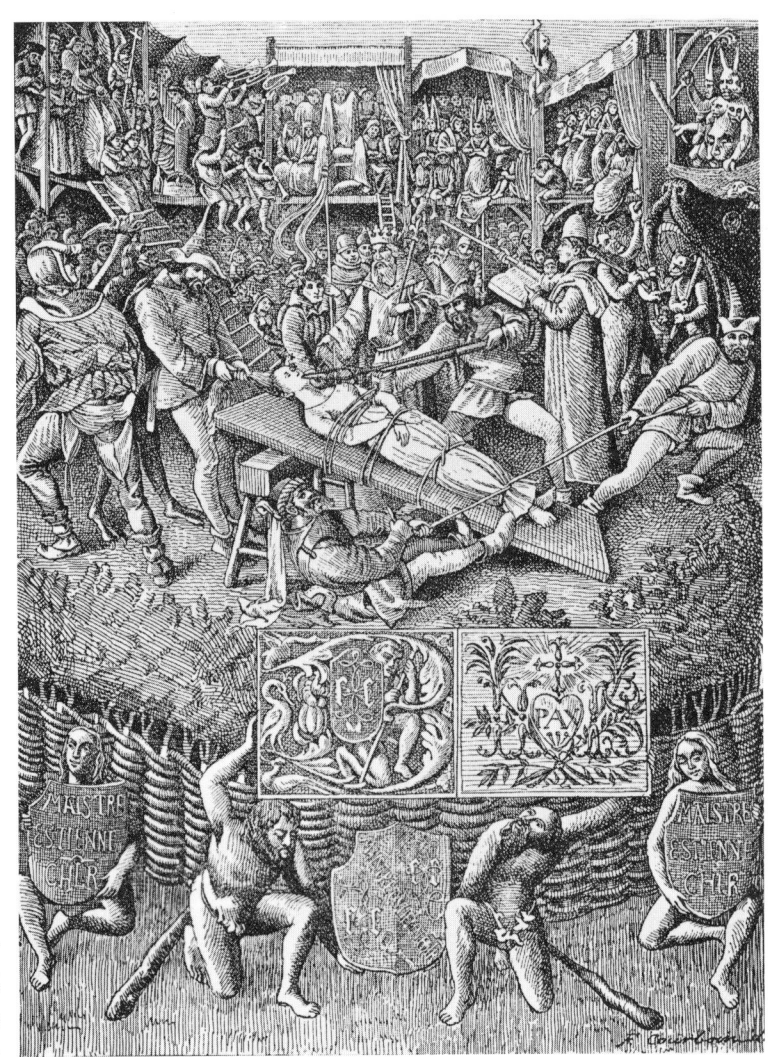

The rehearsal of a 15th-century mystery play, 'The Martyrdom of St. Apollonia'. Notice the director with book.

pictures and from copies of a few of the plays and accounts of their production. We know, for instance, that while God the Father was paid 2s a day for his acting and the devils only 1s 6d, Herod earned 4s because his raging was so strenuous.

History of the British theatre

Elizabethan and Jacobean drama

We fly on now to the reigns of Elizabeth I (1558–1603) and James I (1603–25). At the beginning of that time strolling players were performing single plays on trestle stages set up in halls or the courtyards of inns (where spectators could watch from the ground or from the galleries that used to surround the courtyards), or sometimes in arenas used mostly for the baiting of bulls and bears.

In 1576 the first regular English theatre since the time of the Romans was built in London. It was a circular building with a stage attached to one side, the audience watching from the ground or the galleries that ran two thirds of the way round, not unlike the old inn courtyard. Its name was simply The Theatre. This theatre was soon joined by others, the Swan and the Globe among them. The Globe was the playhouse for which Shakespeare wrote many of his plays. See if you can find out the names of three others.

If you discuss early theatres with your English or drama teacher you may be able to work out how it is that we know anything about these Elizabethan playhouses, although none of them is in existence now.

There is still a great deal of argument about how a theatre of that time was arranged. If a time machine could transport us to one, I am sure we should come back with some surprising discoveries.

For instance, do you know why the 'dead' bodies in an Elizabethan play were always carried off the stage during the scene? What was peculiar about the acting of women's parts?

Rogues and Vagabonds?

Certainly the new theatres seemed to inspire a host of talented playwrights. The old religious plays were replaced by historical dramas and sensational tragedies, leading up to the richest collection of tragedies, comedies and histories ever produced by a single dramatist, by William Shakespeare, himself an actor. Puritans thought there was something sinful about the theatre and managed to pass a law declaring actors to be 'rogues and vagabonds'. The Queen and some important men, who enjoyed watching plays, put special companies of actors under their own protection. Thus Shakespeare belonged at one time to 'The Lord Chamberlain's Men'. Try to discover the name of another such Elizabethan acting company.

Far from being rogues or vagabonds Shakespeare and others made respectable fortunes in the theatre. The actor Edward Alleyn founded the famous school which still exists at Dulwich. There were also popular clowns (we would call them comedians) such as Tarleton who made his audience roar with laughter by wearing boots and breeches too big for him and pushing his hat into funny shapes.

The playhouses were described as stately and sumptuous. With the audience on three sides of the stage there could not be scenery in the ordinary sense, but lists of properties from the old Rose Theatre prove to us that the stage was not as bare as used to be supposed. It includes the city of Rome, the cloth of the Sun and Moon and the tomb of Dido.

Masques and Puritans

Towards the end of this time masques became a favourite pastime at Court. These were entertainments made up of song, recitation, dance and spectacle devised to do honour to important guests. The words were by well-known poets, the music by distinguished musicians and the elaborate sets and costumes by gifted artists, Inigo Jones in particular.

The actors, however, were amateurs. James I's queen herself often took part and so did Charles I when he was a boy. Enormous sums were spent on magnificent clothes and splendid scenery. Once a single performance cost £10,000, which, of course, would be worth far more in today's money.

Masques were the ancestors of opera and ballet but, except for great advances in scenic effect, they had little influence on straight theatre.

When the Puritans came to power in 1649 they closed all the theatres. If any actors were discovered performing in secret they were liable to be flogged and the audience was fined five shillings a head.

History of the British theatre

The 'Restoration' and after

The new theatres that opened after Charles II returned as king in 1660 were quite different from the earlier ones and more like our own. They were much influenced by Italy and France. Most of the stage was now set behind a proscenium, although a large forestage or 'apron' still remained in front of it. Complicated painted scenery with deep perspectives was all the fashion. Actresses instead of boy actors now played women's parts and frivolous comedies of manners were very popular.

This reign saw the foundation in London of two theatres licensed by the King. One was Lincoln's Inn Fields, the other still exists. What is its name? The building was burnt down several times before the present one was put up on the same site. Do you know what made old theatres so liable to fires?

Design by Inigo Jones for costume of Penthesileia in The Masque of Queens.

David Garrick as Macbeth in the 1770s. Notice that he is dressed in the fashion of his own time and not that of Shakespeare or of Macbeth himself.

The most famous actor of the eighteenth century was David Garrick. He came to London to work in the wine trade but he was stage-struck and before long managed to find work in the theatre. His very first big part, that of Richard III, won him enormous success and soon he was the rage of London. His way of acting must have been much more natural than any seen before. Quin, the best known actor before Garrick's appearance, declared 'If he is right, then I and all other actors are wrong.' He improved the theatres in many ways. One reform was to abolish the right of fashionable young men to have seats on the stage itself, as hitherto.

Garrick made a fortune, toured Britain and Europe and when he died in 1779 was buried at the foot of Shakespeare's statue in Westminster Abbey.

Mrs Siddons (1755–1831) was renowned as the greatest of

History of the British theatre

Mrs Siddons, the famous tragic actress, in about 1790.

tragic actresses. Of her it was written, 'Her beautiful face and form, the exquisite tones of her voice, thrilled every soul. Men wept, women fell into hysterics, transports of applause shook the house.' Can you find out the names of two other great actors of about that time?

Programmes of this period show that the night's entertainment lasted a long time and usually included at least a farce and a jig as well as the main play. When gas lighting was introduced into theatres in the mid-nineteenth century it became possible for the first time for an audience to sit in the dark and watch an illuminated stage

The early Victorian theatre laid great stress on famous actors and spectacular scenery but was poor in new plays and intelligent productions of old ones. Production began to improve towards the end of the reign with Sir Henry Irving, the first actor and manager to be knighted.

In spite of a strange appearance and way of speaking, his stage personality was so powerful that the audience was almost hypnotized by him. His partner in most of his vast Shakespearean productions was the lovely Ellen Terry. People said that when she entered a room it was as if the sun came out.

If your project includes the nineteenth-century theatre you should find out about the following famous people: Herbert Beerbohm Tree, Mrs Patrick Campbell and Gordon Craig.

By the time the twentieth century had arrived the theatre was seething with new ideas about production, design and acting. Plays such as those of Ibsen in Norway and George Bernard Shaw in England were startling their audiences into new thinking. And the theatre of today continues to experiment.

Do-it-yourself theatre 9

Amateur dramatic companies
How to set about producing a play and acting in it
Making costumes and scenery from very little

All this time we have been discussing the professional theatre, but most of you may find it difficult to penetrate that world, possibly because there is no such theatre in your neighbourhood. In most places, however, there are amateur dramatic societies. Some are very small and far from expert, but even from them something can be learned, and several well-known professional actors started in that way. There are other amateur groups that have a great deal of experience and put on very good shows. It is a great step forward when they can acquire their own headquarters with a stage, perhaps in an adapted barn or similar building, instead of hiring a hall for a day or two. A few companies have even erected excellent small modern theatres of their own after enormous fund-raising efforts.

Amateur drama cannot be expected to reach the level of professional theatre because those concerned in the latter undergo long training, are in constant practice and depend on it for their living. At worst, amateur productions give some understanding of the art of the theatre and a great deal of pleasure to the company.

How to start
If you are interested in any branch of the theatre, why not seek out your nearest amateur society and join it? These groups often need help in other ways as well as with acting. Or it may be that you would like to have a go at producing an entertainment yourselves. If you have the keenness and grit to see it through,

it will help you to know a great deal more about the theatre and be enormous fun at the same time.

I am sure any teacher who produces plays will help you with advice. The foregoing pages mostly apply to the amateur as much as to the professional stage, but here are a few extra tips for beginners.

Choose a short but good play — then it will be interesting even if the acting is weak!

There will be a number of decisions to make before you can start. Whether you all join in or elect a committee, do find out about committee rules first. They will save you from those frustrating meetings where everyone talks at once, wanders from subject to subject without settling anything and then forgets what was decided in the end.

Members of the cast must agree not to argue with the director while rehearsing. The director must be prepared to discuss points with the cast at the end of each rehearsal.

Amateurs may need more precise direction than professionals do. Whether he follows the directions in the acting edition or invents his own, the director must plot positions and movements clearly in advance. It will be useful to draw a plan of the stage with squares marked upstage right (from the actor's point of view), centre, left centre etc. on which moves can be worked out with buttons representing the actors. Inter-leave the book of the play with lined paper for noting down directions.

If special lighting is used the electrician must make sure that the main supply can carry it and, above all, that the wiring is safe. Ask about fire regulations before you light candles on the stage.

A few hints
Inexperienced actors often lay too equal stress on all words and sentences. Listen to everyday speech. You will find that people do not speak evenly. They emphasize important words, say some phrases quickly and carelessly, hesitate, laugh a little perhaps or pause. As a rule be very quick on cues (your turn to speak) but if a pause is needed do not be afraid to stay silent. Don't fidget about from foot to foot. Relax. Stillness can be very effective.

Do-it-yourself theatre 63

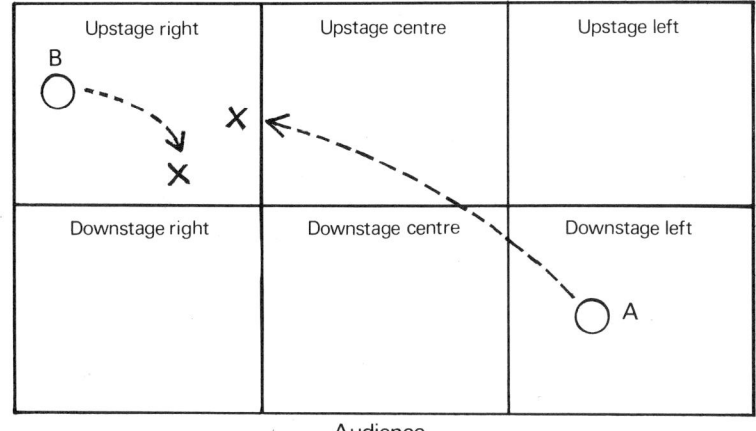

Dividing the stage into imaginary squares for plotting moves (left and right are always from the actor's point of view).

Learn your words as soon as you can. Until you know them really well you cannot begin to act.

When you have difficulty with one of your speeches it sometimes helps to imagine how you would say the same thing in your own words if a comparable situation happened to you.

If you feel horribly nervous before your entrance on the first night — and most actors do — take a deep breath, then breathe out and say to yourself 'Isn't this *fun*?' and sail on to the stage as you breathe in again.

It is fascinating to create scenery and costumes for very little money — lattice bay-windows out of a clothes horse, canvas and black tape, royal thrones from packing cases covered with hessian and trimmed with thick wool fringe, crown jewels from coloured milk tops, decorative masks from breakfast cereal boxes, tissue paper, gummed strip and poster paint.

When planning costumes, design what you want and see how near you can get to it rather than design according to what you have! Beautiful historical robes can be made from old curtains. How the actor wears the costume makes a great difference.

However, you will find a number of splendid books in the public library to help you with all aspects of do-it-yourself theatre.

10 Finance

What the income from selling tickets has to be spent on
Patrons who paid for plays to be produced in past centuries
About patrons today

It is clear that theatres are expensive concerns to build and run. Let us look into their finances.

Find out how many seats there are in an average theatre and how much each kind costs. (There are travel and theatre agents in every town and I think a friendly member of their staff would help you in this if not too busy.) Work out how much money would come in at each performance if the house were full. Now take away a quarter of that sum because a theatre is not always fully booked. If you can bear any more calculations, multiply your answer by the number of performances a week – usually seven or eight counting matinées (afternoon performances). Now you have the weekly income of a fairly successful theatre. It may sound a large amount but there are a great many expenses to be subtracted from it before there can be any profit. The actors and all the stage staff have to be paid, the theatre must be lit and kept in repair, the author of the play takes a small percentage (called a 'royalty') and there is the cost of scenery and costumes to be defrayed. These are not the only expenses. Can you think of other possible items?

As well as all this there is usually a rent to be paid for the theatre. The total expenses have gone up even more quickly than the price of the seats, so you can see that only a really successful entertainment will make a profit. The money needed to start it with is usually provided by a company or individual hoping to gain by it. Often the people who have invested their money in a play – they are called 'backers' – or 'angels' in theatrical slang – lose most of it. No wonder plays with very few

Finance

characters and no change of scenery are so popular nowadays — they are cheaper to produce!

This state of affairs often means that people are afraid to put on plays, however good, unless they are almost sure to be financially successful very soon. Thus many new and interesting plays get left on the shelf because no one dares to risk his money. Ballet and opera are particularly expensive and very likely to run at a loss.

Luckily it is still possible to try out plays that are new or experimental in less expensive theatres, often quite tiny ones, or in university drama societies, etc.

Patrons, old style and new

In the Middle Ages the city councils and trade guilds often paid for the plays that were put on in their town. Later on there were sometimes princes and very rich men and women who were so fond of the arts that they were willing to spend some of their wealth on supporting them. Such people were known as 'patrons', but nowadays they are in short supply. Fortunately the state has stepped into their place.

In 1945 the Arts Council of Great Britain was founded to help all the arts. Its aim is to give grants of money to all artistic ventures that are considered worth while. In its first year it contributed £30,000 towards theatrical enterprises of all kinds. By 1969 the sum was well over £1,000,000 in a year. Perhaps the most famous of all the undertakings it has made possible is the National Theatre.

Sometimes town and county councils too will help towards grants for theatrical ventures in their area.

Where does all this money come from? It comes out of the rates and taxes paid by the people of this country, and that means that a little part of the nation's theatre belongs to you. You should not think of it as money poured out with no financial return, however, Our plays and actors have gained a fine reputation, and every year a great many people come from abroad to visit our theatres, bringing money into the country. More than that, a nation is judged very much by the quality of the art it produces and we want our theatre to be something we can be proud of.

Aids to research and projects on the theatre

In the Introduction there was mention of several theatres that cater for the young by putting on plays especially for them, sending companies round the district to present plays in schools and halls or running an arts centre with all sorts of interesting activities as well as theatre.

There are quite a few more. The theatre at Rhyl in Wales was the first to consider youth in this way. At the Belgrade Theatre in Coventry young people can buy seats at reduced prices and there are interesting Saturday morning theatre sessions, in addition to a youth theatre which they can join. The Belgrade also sends a touring company to perform in primary and secondary schools.

These are only examples. Similar activities exist in a number of repertory theatres throughout the land, Aberdeen, Nottingham, Sheffield and Watford among them.

If you need information write to the Drama Adviser, c/o the Education Office in your county town. He may also be able to help you if you live too far from the nearest theatre to be able to visit it.

If you write to private individuals it is polite to enclose a stamped-addressed envelope. You are also more likely to get a reply to your enquiry.

Some useful books

The following reference books, almost certainly in your public library, should prove useful:
The Oxford Companion to the Theatre (general theatrical information)
Who's Who in the Theatre (living theatrical personalities)
The Dictionary of National Biography (celebrities of the past)
The Encyclopaedia Britannica
The Oxford Dictionary
On the shelves there will probably be a selection of books on various aspects of the theatre. Here are some titles:
The Development of the Theatre by Allardyce Nicoll, Harrap.
Staging the Play by N. Lambourne, Studio Vista.
First Steps in Acting by S. Seldon, Owen.
Theatrical Costume and the Amateur Stage by Michael Green, Arco Publications.
Stage Lighting by Geoffrey Ost, Herbert Jenkins.
There are also journals devoted entirely to the theatre, such as *The Stage* and *Plays and Players*.

Glossary of technical terms used

Apron stage: part of stage in front of proscenium, jutting out into the audience.
Backdrop: stretched scenic cloth concealing the whole back wall of the stage.
Batten: bar hanging over the stage and usually fitted with lights.
Border: flat piece of scenery or short curtain stretching across above the stage from one side to the other.
Box set: a 3-sided set representing a room.
Cast: all the actors in a play.
Cyclorama ('Cyc'): plain curved wall or cloth at the back of the stage.
Downstage: the front of the stage, the part nearest to the audience.
Elevation: scale drawing of a building seen vertically without perspective.
Flats: flat pieces of scenery made by stretching canvas on a wooden frame.
Flies: space above the stage where scenery is hung till wanted.
Footlights (*or Floats*): a row of lights concealed in a shallow trench along the front of the stage.
Gelatine (*or Cinemoid*): transparent slide, usually coloured, inserted in front of stage lights.
Grid: the structure high up in the flies that carries all the ropes and pulleys.
Ground plan: scale drawing of land or building at ground level as seen from directly above.
Ground row: flat piece of scenery running across the floor of the stage.
Improvisation: a performance done without any preparation.
Masking: hiding another actor from view by standing in front of him.
Masques: a court entertainment of great magnificence, popular in the sixteenth and seventeenth centuries.

Glossary of technical terms used

Mystery plays: plays on religious subjects acted in the Middle Ages.
Proscenium: the arch that frames the front of the stage.
Repertory company ('Rep'): a theatrical company acting several plays turn and turn about during a whole season. Also a company that presents plays for two or three weeks only, one after the other.
Rostrum: a raised platform, often foldable.
Sight-lines: imaginary lines defining the limits of the field of vision.
Strip: a row of stage lights.
Upstage: the back of the stage, the part furthest from the audience.
Wings: the sides of the stage, out of sight of the audience.
Wing-flats: pieces of scenery projecting from the wings.

Acknowledgments

The author and publishers would like to thank those listed below for permission to reproduce illustrations:

Anthony Crickmay; The Devonshire Collection, Chatsworth, for the illustration of the design by Inigo Jones. Reproduced by permission of the Chatsworth Settlement Trustees; The Raymond Mander and Joe Mitchenson Theatre Collection; The National Theatre Company; The Nottingham Playhouse; The Octagon Theatre, Bolton; Photograph of stage with lighting equipment by courtesy of Rank Strand Electric Ltd; The Royal Shakespeare Company; Photograph of Maggie Smith and Robert Stephens by courtesy of 20th Century Fox Film Company; John Vickers; The Victoria and Albert Museum.

The author gratefully acknowledges the help of Mr André van Gyseghem.